A FARING LIFE

EXPERIENCES, ADAPTING AND SELF - DISCOVERY

YIMKUMER

I dedicate this book to my "Oba" (dad) for always loving me. I have never thanked you enough. But your love, support, sacrifice, and dedication towards me and my brother for all these years have never been overlooked. I thank you for being the man behind everything I am today.

Contents

Contents

About The Author

The author is a Generation Z, born in a small village in Nagaland, away from the cities hustle & bustle. Apart from writing books, he enjoys making art & cooking. A modest, humble and broad-minded person, who tries to grasp and learn from everyday experiences.

A Faring Life is his first debut book. He has the advantage of his own company, musing most of his time. He is also someone who runs in search of a pen and paper if some interesting thoughts cross his mind or try not to let slip, just to note it down later.

Of himself he write persuasively yes; Putting thoughts and experiences lesson into a book to share with the help of his pen and paper is harder than he thought and more rewarding than he could have ever envision.

You can connect with the author at:

Instagram: authoryimkum

Email- yimkumlkr920@gmail.com

Preface

This book has been an aspiration not just to bring this "book" a reality but to share my learning experiences, to look at things from different perspectives, and letting every phase of life be a learning experience. I always wanted to share my perspective on different things and most importantly I wanted to preserve my wisdom in the form of this book. That's how it all started. This has been one of the most challenging experience in my life thus, far kicking off with zero experience in writing a book to putting all efforts, knuckling down to something which I really thought about for a long time. A lot more has been faced; from the very first day I started investing my time into this book, from doubting myself, thoughts like am I capable enough to write a book and a lot more. Beating against all odds, here is a little commemoration to call this book "A book of mine".

I had two choices, either speak out or remain mumb to the voices inside my head. I believe we are all capable of doing the things we love, whatever the cases maybe. I don't intend to portray myself as the perfect being by any means, nor are my writings/thoughts to be universally true. This book is only an unveiling of my knowledge and experience with people whoever choose to read, as I believe that words can travel far and has the power to impact and change people's lives.

Acknowledgements

First and Foremost, I would like to thank my readers for choosing this book. Significant thoughts and innumerable hours have been invested into this book. I am so thankful to almighty God, the author of all wisdom and knowledge, for leading me this far with His countless love and for being the source of my strength throughout this journey.

"No book is one person's effort alone". For this one too, I extend my heartfelt gratitude to Ms. Tiaenla Pongen and Mr. Imlikokba Kichu for their efforts and time in polishing every word in the book. Also, my sincere gratitude to Mr. Sosangmar Jamir for being a wonderful editor for my book cover. A simple thank you is not enough to express my gratitude towards your contributions. Thank you for being there.

I also would like to extent my gratitude to each and every individual who have dedicated their priceless time, energy and wisdom, whose names are not enumerated. Your contributions are eminently acknowledged.

I am also thankful to the Notion Press Publishing Team for supporting me and venturing in publishing this book. Last but not the least I would also like to thank Vishal Ved for his guidance & support.

My heartfelt gratitude to all whoever has contributed in the completion of this book.

God Bless.

CHAPTER ONE

Create Your own Reality

Our assumption of the world is usually the cosmos that surrounds us. Reality is not a fictitious imagination but, it is something objective that can be seen and felt. There is world out there; the world that affects your mood, emotions, feelings etc., even the weather affects your mood both physically and mentally.

Alongside this reality, there is an inner reality in which you truly live. This inner world is as much real and occurring as the outer world, but you have no much control of events that take place in the outer world. Yet you are very much in control of your inner world. You can mould your inner world and create a reality of your own. Inner reality consists of your patterns of thoughts, feelings, response to things and situations. Even the myths and superstitions constitutes your reaction to certain circumstances. This inner reality of yours really clasp you fast, but still you are the master of it, and you have the authority to control, shape and modify it. Your happiness and sadness in life depends on your inner reality. Perhaps you can be mistreated by the people you love but still be happy and forgive them. It is absolutely your choice and within your control to react either violently or gracefully.

It is important to remember that your emotions, feelings, reactions and actions are real. You are living in this inner reality as much as in your outer reality. You have the power to adapt by choosing thoughts that are positive and true by eliminating negative feelings, beliefs in myths and superstitions. Even if the outer world is not pleasing to you, your inner reality should be strongly based, so that you can live happily and peacefully.

Your inner reality, your feelings, emotions and belief system is your reality, the lone reality in which you truly live. So it is very important for you to know your true self fully. It can be terrible if you do not understand yourself and who you truly are.

CHAPTER TWO

Life is not all chance

Life is stormy, none can escape it. At the point of death, the only thing people regret about is not the things they have done, but the things they could have done when they had the opportunity and the things taken for granted.

Most people fail to see that a man's mind is the man himself as in, You create the world and the environment you live in. At some point you will be surprised to learn that everything about you is pretty much the way you create it. Life is not by chance; instead a matter of choice. The way you live is the result of the choices you make, as no matter who you are, what you have or don't, you are given the choices and you are defined by the choices you made. If you could make your choice and shape the reality you live in today, you can also change your mind-set, choose a fresh choice and alter your life situation.

When you realise that your mind can create your world, you are the master of your life from then on. Everyone stumbles at some point and that's when we are given an opportunity to become stronger. However, we often fail to understand our weaknesses and start limiting ourselves which is actually dangerous and regretful. If you fail to rise again, your self-understood limitations can sometimes imprison your truself.

Believe that you are made to achieve great things, have faith to achieve the impossible. You are free to build your beliefs, establish your attitudes and follow your passion with trust and inner intuition.

When life is good, do not take it for granted as it will pass. Be mindful, compassionate and cherish the good moments. Above all, in this fast growing world, be a HUMAN.

CHAPTER THREE

It's okay to feel things differently

There is no limit to how we feel. You and I feel differently for different reasons. You cannot control the feelings of other people nor do they have control over your feelings.

They say feelings cannot be suppressed nor can they be denied. Then what must one do with his feelings? Is feeling everything deeply a blessing or a curse? We often seek answers to such questions out of curiosity and there is nothing wrong with that sensation. To answer such queries, one can only share from one's point of view, which everyone may not appreciate or accept. However, it depends on which side you are and what you choose to feel. Some consider it a blessing to feel everything deeply, while others consider it a curse.

More often, I have seen people who feel so deeply are selfless. They try to understand the person's woe and provide every possible support. In some cases, I have witnessed people putting everything at stake to support the ones struggling in life. Consequently, I have seen people who are always happy to get help from those compassionate people and enjoy being taken care by them.

However, when these compassionate people need a helping hand, it is not readily available to them. Rather, they would be mocked at with tags such as "fragile", "overthinker" and many more. And there are some people instead of being a helping hand, enjoys watching someone's misery, as if their miseries is something entertaining for them.

Everyone needs to understand and be there for each other, as we never know when will setbacks and misfortunes may come knocking at the door every once in a while. We have to learn and understand how to deal with our own feelings and on the other hand, one must also acknowledge people's feelings and respect what they feel and go through.

CHAPTER FOUR

Put yourself out there

If you never step up and set yourself into the things you love, you will never know what's up there, and how it feels like to be. Nothing or no one can guarantee you at your best or your worst, but it's only when you put yourself and start taking your own pace. By trying all the things you always wanted to, you actually win over your fears and you get to learn something you know nothing about.

Life is about being practically facing up all the high and lows, it's also full of ventures, defeat, discouragement and achievements and that's what makes life beautiful, and precious.

Life can end at anytime. It might be tomorrow, next week, or in a year from now but, it will. As that's the destiny of all kind. You never know when and how life will snatch you away. So, live up your life to the fullest, fight all your fears, try everything you've always wanted to, have courage to pursue even if you fail after all, what better way is there to live.

You might be well prepared, knowing it well in advance or go out in a blink of an eye but even if you live up to a ripe old age and is well prepared, looking back it will surely seems that life went by incredibly quick. Life is too short not to go for what you desire so, don't wait to happen instead work for it and make it happen. It's too late and you're too old to keep waiting any longer.

Stop prolonging; stop hoping that things will change tomorrow or that you will stumble upon what you love eventually.

Stop looking for a perfect partner to magically appear or that you'll meet eyes across the street with your true love soon.

Stop all your wishes and hopes instead, start taking life into your hands, because it might not happen in time. But if you only put yourself there, facing and working towards it, putting your time, energy and dedication, if only you try your best and have faith, you at least increase your chances of getting what you wanted. It may not happen the way you want, but you are not betting on just chance.

Take a look at your dreams and the things you always wanted to do. Don't be afraid of rejection and downfall instead, ask yourself, whose dream is it? And who's gonna work for it? What you have done in past years and days to achieve that? Did you really give everything you have? Would you be able to say that you feel proud of what you did if you were to die tomorrow? Or would you feel you missed out? Or you ought to regret for all the things for not trying your best.

You will find your answer then eventually.

Remember that, "Regret is the only word that makes you regret". Many of us still go through life as if we were to live forever even though we know we are not, I know this is all horrible clinch to write out but maybe that's the excuse why few people actually sit down and think about it.

I know you think this is being said already way too much about "putting yourself out there and facing your fears". I know everyone logically understands it, but it must be really getting it.

May be it won't change anything, but may be you will find the courage to jump over your own shadow and start living up all your fears and overcome them one after the other and help someone out there too instead of hoping for chance.

CHAPTER FIVE

Truth about Self-esteem

When I was young, I had a very clear notion about what was truth and what was not, what was good and what wasn't. My answers then were prompted "yes" or "no". But as I grew older, I've seen and heard so many events in life that it has become very difficult for me to say 'yes' or 'no' to every question, often there is an answer but left unspoken. But maybe that's how we've grown old and learn as we go on living. I too realised that the perspective of life and even the definition of love and way of seeing things and understanding changes from here to there.

I always wanted to study what really lies behind everything that happens. As we all have different opinion and way of envisioning things, I believe that it's all up to us on how we see things, how we take it to overcome them, enjoy it or grief over it. So, from my point of view, self-esteem doesn't really exist for a person who doesn't believe it, on the flip side it exist for those who believe. But we can't deny anyone's perception, as I mention earlier we all see and take things differently.

I too opine and hold that the cold truth about self – esteem is, it doesn't exist, as it's only within us. So it all depends on us on how we react, deal with it and how we assume if there is or there isn't. It's just something we wend. And it's not just one particular individual but many others too.

It is based on the image that "I should feel good about myself all the time", "I should always be happy", "beautiful", "always be at the top" etc. that one desires for something beyond one have. But what is this idea and notion based on, if we try to perceive truly? Basically, it boils down to "feeling content and happy feels good" so, I want to feel in such way always. That's it. That's the doctrine and believes. And that's the problem with it, because if you think a little bit deeper and that you've already made up your mind that you should always feel good, happy and beyond, you can't accept the negative thoughts and thus, it becomes the problem. Whenever you feel bad and low you feel like you're doing something wrong that your life isn't working as it should be the way you thought and expect and all of this contributes to your low self-esteem.

The fact is we all can confirm this simply by examining our own way of life that, life doesn't always treats you well, it was never meant to be and it's an inevitable part of life. You're going to have a bad day, slip and fall, stub your toe, eat something that upsets your stomach, get rejected by someone you love, lost someone very dear to you or simply wake up feeling blue. But there's nothing wrong with any of that. Therefore, the moment you realise that feeling low is entirely normal and natural part of life; and every issue you once considered a problem stop being a problem.

You can try and fail, you can do everything right but still fall short, you can feel insecure about some sort of things but that's just the way life is and that is how you learn, grow and become stronger.

The amazing things about life is that, when you stop turning a temporary bad feeling into a problem, that bad feeling will last till it no longer exist. Most issues that needs a solution are actually just temporary bad feelings so, it is better sometimes to just go with the flow or let it go, as they are just natural feelings, emotions that every individual go through and thus, you don't have to keep repressing them over and over again for the rest of your life. So, trust the process and just take your own pace one day at a time and you will eventually realise that you are free to be as you are without constantly thinking about yourself and your problems. From that instance, one's – esteem and emotions will no longer be an idea that seems burden and extremely applicable.

CHAPTER SIX

Yin and Yang in Life

Pain and pleasure is not the thing that happens to you, it's not that it comes knocking with time. It's true that everything changes with time, but that doesn't mean you got to forget things, because there are things that leaves a scar even when the wound is healed long ago. There are moments and feeling we still finds it fresh and makes us aware, as if it's still present inside us as it lingers within us. Everything that happens, your happiness, sorrow, your pain & pleasure is not part of life but its life itself and that's what makes life beautiful and more truce.

Life is a blend of good and bad things, pain & pleasure, rainy and sunny, joy and grief, success and failure, it's full of ups and downs. There is an Arab proverbs that says "sunshine all the day makes a desert", but rain is as important as sunshine as the earth cannot support life without water. So in order to know the things you don't know, you have to go through a lot to know what you really want to know and what you really want to get it done.

We are so much into worldly pleasure that we only appreciate good things and most often we fail to take an account of the immense joy that surrounds us and the life we are living. Waking up every morning is a privilege, those beautiful flowers, plants, hills and the valleys, the field and the meadows all that surround us offers a beautiful picture, views and sound for us. There are many valid reasons for us to be thankful but we fail to see all of these and never consider it as blessings.

Life is not as bad as you think. You will find more reason to be happy than sorrow if you take account of all the little things. But we get focused on few pain and failure that, we completely shut to see good things that happen around us.

Remember that, the best thing about life is that everything you lost has replaced you with something better and everything you are losing now and has yet to lose will be replaced by something way more better. It's just that we fail to see as we only focus on what we've lost, but if we only try to look back and reflect, we will find that what we achieve is far more greater than what we didn't envisioned for ourselves.

CHAPTER SEVEN

Don't take anything for granted

Life is a beautiful journey, it's a gift full of blessings at the same time life is also very much unpredictable. One moment something is yours, and the other moment it is snatched away. You only know the true importance of something only after losing it. Currently this is a general human tendency and may vary.

Learn to appreciate the things and people you have. Do not ever have the mindset of "forever mine" and take it easy. And if you do not respect what you have, you will realise its value only after losing them. Always be thankful for everything you have. Mourning over the loss that you've once taken for granted is one of the most painful experiences you will ever come across. There are so many beautiful things in life we take for granted without realising that we should be thankful for them. Realising you have the opportunity to live them, never let it go. The things you have right now might be a dream for many.

Do not assume that you are going to wake up tomorrow and things will be up to the mark just because that has been the case every day. For life can go upside down in a second at any given moment. You could die from random probabilities you've never imagined. Hence, embrace and appreciate everything and make the most of it, because that is all you are guaranteed. Appreciate the people around you as it is rare to have people around you that love, care and support you. There are people who regret the last words spoken to someone while some never get the chance to actually voice out their feelings.

We think we have the time, we think to ourselves that there will be another new day or a chance to be around people we love until we realise that they are no longer with us. Do not take anything for granted, as we never know how long they will be there for us. They might love you but they will not always be around, they might be yours to keep today however forever cannot be assured. When you realize the value of someone, you learn to truly appreciate and treasure the people around you.

Always take care of what you have and tell people how you actually feel, as opportunities are taken away in a blink of an eye, but regret lasts for a lifetime.

"Embrace what you have before it slips away".

CHAPTER EIGHT

Observe to learn

May I engage you in a true story that I have experienced, that have taught me great life lessons?

When I was a little boy, I observed that my dad had a lot of friends around him. His friends often visited our house and had a great time. They even brought liquor at times, got drunk together and went out until midnight. I had no idea about what they were doing. All I knew and thought was my dad was a lucky person to have such great companions beside him.

As a little boy, I really liked his friends because they always brought me candies, toys, and stuffs that all kids liked. This was a time when my dad was earning sufficiently to provide us a stable life. All the while, I envied my dad and his friends and wished to find friends like them.

As I grew older, I noticed that my dad's friends were no longer around him. It was unfortunate for my dad as things started to change. He started losing things he loved, slowly even lowered his incomes that led us to misery. Because we ran out of money, I failed to see many old faces and almost all of his friends who were there back then. I wondered why they never visited us. I was curious for an answer but had none to share and ask about it. I started to question myself and tried to find answers to every question I put up with myself.

As I was still immature to understand, I had no concept of fake people and fake friends. Later, I learned about that from my dad's life. As years passed, I eventually realised that the day you lose everything and something close to you, is the day you will know who your real friends are and who really cares about you.

I am glad that I have at least learned a harsh truth through my observations and it was worth it. This has been one of the thousands of life lessons I have acquired. Also, this has been one of the most valuable lessons I have learned so far.

Summing up, I have learned that, in life you have to start choosing yourself first. Do not depend on others for life to work out because at the end of the day, it is you alone that will bear all obstacles in life. The people you trusted for years can make you feel unwanted and abandon you in just a day. In the same way, some people can make you feel so much loved and wanted, which a person normally in years could not do. So love the people who treat you right, forgive the ones who do not, and stay connected with those people who brings out the best in you.

CHAPTER NINE

Love knows no limitations

We hardly find people who can cross skies, get to the moon or become rich and successful just to prove one's love. If you love the person because he/she changes, would you still love them if they changed in other ways? Or do you love the person because of what they possess? Wouldn't that love be lost if they lost possession of those?

The promises of giving heaven on earth will not last because everything on its own course of time will come to an end one day. We submit ourselves in love although the promises of getting everything in the world for your loved ones are not always valid. We cannot bend another's ego and we cannot get a soul at will.

People who truly love each other will go to any extent to express their love for each other. In fact there are many individuals who sacrifice their future and well being for the sake of their loved ones. They are always there for each other. Where there is love, nothing is too high or low, no sacrifice too small, no burden too heavy; wives giving up everything for their husband, lovers sacrificing for their partners, parents sacrificing everything for their children. Also, we come across people surrendering towards love, exceeding the norms of one's own kin and kind.

Love is a mighty emotion. Many believe it does not exists. Many assume that it is fictional or something you can only dream about. However, I beg to differ. Love is not only in films or stories. It is actually a part of life unless it is divided by caste, creed, religion, colour and beyond. Love can be blind and unreasonable. This at times can be the cause of destruction for many youngsters. When in love, people rush themselves without finding a reason or purpose yet end up in a game or fantasy.

Once a sparrow fell in love with a white rose. However, the rose rejected his proposal and told him that only when the rose turns red, it will love him back. The sparrow was willing, however, it was not easy for him to turn the rose into red. The sparrow found a sharp thorn and poked himself. He spread his blood on the white rose, turning it red. The rose fell in love with the sparrow until he as was no more.

Here we learnt that when everything is said and done, grief is the price we pay for love.

This simple story is so profound and thought provoking but it is true that we only know the value of love when it no longer exists. We see that we lose so many beautiful souls in the name of love. Love knows no limitations. It is just a word until someone comes along and shows us its true meaning. It takes forever to really proof love to be true. Love and forever together are just mere words unless it is proven by actions.

CHAPTER TEN

Value of time

Isn't it ironic people wake up every day, go about their daily routines and activities repeatedly and expect the outcome to be different? Everyone talks about time but only few talks about its value and make the best use of it. There is a misconception when talking about the idea of time; we think that it is people wasting our time when actually we ourselves are wasting our time. It is our fault if we think that people are wasting our time because in practice, we choose to spend our time with people and things we love and care. We usually tend to ignore the ones that we least care and love.

Don't let someone be a priority in your life when you are to them is just an option. Some of us lose people that are most important to us because we don't appreciate and value their efforts and time. We don't realise the importance of someone until they are no longer around. We ignore the ones that care about us until they get hurt even more for loving us.

There are two different voices that lives and feed within us. The first voice wants to uplift us, spend quality time with people that care about us. Then there is this second voice that holds us back, a voice that makes you feel that you have enough time. From the moment we open our eyes till the moment we go to bed, there is these two voices battling inside of us and guess who wins? The voice we choose to listen to, the one we choose to feed. It all depends on us whichever voice we listen to and make use of our time.

When asked what is the biggest mistake we make in life? Buddha replied, "The biggest mistake is, you think you have time". And I think that short phrase is powerful enough to answer the question. Time teaches us the value of life. Time is free but it is priceless. You cannot own it but you can use it, you cannot pause it, yet you can spend it. Once you lose it, you can never get it back. Time is more valuable than money and status, as money and status can be earned. Time once lost cannot be regained. Time teaches us two things - Nothing is permanent and Life moves on.

Imagine there is a bank that credits your account each morning with Rs 86,400, however, it does not allow you to keep such balance. What would you do? Anyone would withdraw every penny of course and make the best use of it. Every single day we get deposited Eighty Six Thousand Four Hundred seconds of time into our life. However, knowingly or unknowingly, we waste it. I don't think anyone would ever waste it unnecessarily if it was actual money. So the question here is, when it comes to time, why do we waste it? If we are to think about it, a second is so much greater and more powerful than money because money can always be earned, while time is priceless.

There is a famus quote written by a famous French author, Mar Levy, which says, "If you want to know the value of one year, just ask a student who failed a course".

"If you want to know the value of one month, ask a mother who gave birth to a premature baby".

"If you want to know the value of one hour, ask the lovers waiting to meet".

"If you want to know the value of one minute, ask the person who just missed the bus".

"If you want to know the value of one second, ask the person who just escaped death in a car accident".

"And if you want to know the value of one-hundredth of a second, ask the athlete who won a silver medal in the Olympics".

Many of us do not realise the value of time until it has passed. It is saddening to think that humans tend to care for the things they have only after losing its value and are out of reach. Existence and time are the best two preceptors in our life as existence teaches us to make good use of time and time teaches us the value of time.

CHAPTER ELEVEN

Living your true-self

If we look at the people around us, we see so many beautiful and bright faces; little do we know what one is going through. We may only see what a person choose to show us; likewise, another person will only get to see what we choose to show. If we reciprocate and only spent time to find answers, there's always a reason and most often the reasons begins with "inability of self-acceptance in areas most commonly, physical appearance and most interestingly for being different from others are the bedrock.

Often, we are asked to socialize and we are told not to be too quite, or to stop daydreaming, when actually that is who we truly are, how we grow and love ourselves. In between living your life, to conditioning your life to please somebody else, we often end up trying to fit somewhere else, somewhere we don't belong. You and I cannot be somebody else just to fit into the picture because there is no denial that none can play your role better than yourself. Our authenticity is who we really are deep down. You have to be yourself, be proud of who and what you are because at the end of the day, every being is different and that differences is what makes you unique, powerful, capable and functional.

Remember that no one will ever see or feel you as much as you see and feel yourself. For this reason, it is vital to validate yourself no matter what people say or how hard your experiences are. You are wasting your time and energy if you are unhappy about what you don't have or if you are trying to be someone you aren't. The best thing you can do is to be real you despite all the odds. Believe it or not, once you truly accept your flaws and imperfections, there are certain things and elements you cannot change and accept things as it is, that is when you realise happiness lies within you.

So be content and stay true to yourself by accepting all your flaws and imperfections. Every person has strengths and weaknesses. Cultivate the strengths and address the weaknesses, be enthusiastic towards life and confront yourself to positive outlook in life.

From my perspective, a person is truly admirable when he/she possess a generous heart and qualities such as honesty, loyalty, humble and kind. It is not always about the physical appearances or how fat your purse is, or how disingenuous you can be. Be true of who you are, above all, be true to truth.

Never compare your star with someone else' sparks because we all learn, grow and shine at our own pace.

CHAPTER TWELVE

Two Lives

In everyone's life at one's given time, there comes a period of darkness and distress. One feels pressed down, fully depleted and depressed. It is in these moments when one feels that there is no more hope for tomorrow, purpose, reason to live; until one determines to get up from the ground and walk into life once again. Perhaps, this is how one experience depression. No one can escape from it.

As you retrospect your own life, you are burdened with guilt for what you did and what you have failed to do. You wake up suddenly in the middle of the night searching for relief from mental turmoil, fear and regret. You feel like running away from this world and hide yourself forever from the rest of the people hoping to escape from the misery you are in. You feel like you have no one that cares about you and neither you to care for. You become incapable of loving anyone, you stop loving the things you love, your near and dear ones have no meaning for you. The only desire you have is to simply disappear from this place, or try all things to find a way to end your life, to find peace. This is depression at its worst.

If we look closely, today we are constantly loosing people to depression and mental health. We have really reached a point where we should teach people to love themselves and value life. It is time we talk about the cause and effects of depression and other mental health issues. We should stop passing comments such as "be a man", don't cry", "stop being childish". Rather, it is time we start reaching out and help all those individuals who have already lost their hopes on living and has forgotten the priceless gift of life.

How amazing that everyone can put up masks' that aren't theirs actually, it seems like everyone fake having the time they spent with people they are with. Most of us don't really understand what's really going inside in our mind and keep it to ourselves and this is same for others. People will never understand until they have been through that stage.

What we think often while speaking about depression is, we assume that depression is distress; we think that it's about crying alone, we picture that it's about being quite and reserve without wanting people's company. But depression is not something we can see through, or something we can learn from people who have been through that stage, as it's never the same in every two person who go through the depression.

Depression is when we smile at everything but deep inside we cry. It's when we share our feelings and emotions that we are struggling with, knowing that there are somethings that people can't really help and heal you the way you wanted them to.

It's when we talk about it but we want to be quite.

It's when we are present in flesh but our mind is elsewhere.

It's when we pretend we are happy but we actually aren't.

It's when we stop loving the things we love.

Depression is not always true, it's not as you think it seems, it is also not about what we see, but it's about what we don't even think about. Every mental health problem is funny to observe because it's childish, we cry, we avoid people until one get up at that very stage truly and get to know exactly how it feels. Isn't that amazing how we think we know so much of someone and still don't know them at all? I don't think we truly understand how traumatic it is to explain what we feel and what's really going on inside our mind when we don't even understand ourselves.

All of us go through depression, loneliness, anxiety and other mental health issues and difficulties. Lives two sides of life; the life we go through which no one notices and the one which everyone knows about but not actually true, as people and individuals can only know about you which you choose to show them. All of us have been with people in crowd but felt lonely and depressed and wanted to leave, all of us have so many followers, commenter's, liker's, in social platforms but don't have real followers and friends in our real life. All of us have friends and people who know us but don't actually know who we really are but at times we have been alone but felt safe, peace and comfortable too.

It's very important that someone know how you really feel and what you really go through, and that someone starts with you, by knowing your true intention by yourself first. It's important that we spent quality time face to face, it's okay to have a lot of friends who follows you but it's more important to make sure that you have true real friends. Don't live for the approval of others instead live your true self and stay true to yourself. And start connecting with people who looks like your future than your past and start living one original life by starting to love yourself.

CHAPTER THIRTEEN

Truth reveals itself

Throughout life's journey, I have come across diverse people as co-passengers, people from different religion and community. With some I was able to strike up conversations and didn't feel the burden to stay connected. At the same time, some people were complex and hard to associate with. Some people manifestly try to find out who or what am I; some step up into prying hence, I turn defensive. I confuse them with answers that are imprecise. For whatever the reason maybe, when I leave people with no surety, I feel that I have not done my best. However, I affirm myself believing some things must be kept within myself and it is not really necessary people need to know them.

All of us encounter different types of individuals in our life that gives us sorrow, happiness and memories that can be bitter or sweeten our life. Some people are like the clouds, they are beautiful to look at. They bring different colours and mesmerising views and get your attention. They are beautiful at the beginning but eventually they cast away with the flow of the wind. They change their direction with time. When we think of this, we can recall the people that are comparable with the clouds in our journey of life. We must accept the fact that they brought and showed different dimensions of characters in an individual. We must appreciate for the good lessons as well as the bad that helped us in our growth overtime.

Most of the people say “Trust me; I am always here for you”. And so we trust them directly or indirectly, only to find out that all those assurance were just empty words. Often, such people can fool you with their words just as the weather disappoints you with its sudden change.

As we walk through our life, we meet people that teach us certain lessons. Among all the lessons, the best lessons are those when people hurt, betray and use us only for their ulterior motive. However, there are also a handful of people who will be always by our side no matter what the situation may be; those people are like the sky. They support, encourage and believe in us. When you come across such people, hold on to them and treasure them.

Reflect on this: who is the Cloud, Weather or the Sky in your life and vice versa.

With time you learn everything you need; you get to know who someone truly is, you get to learn why some things are just the way it is. It only takes some time to know or understand everything truly. So be patient and know when to let go and whom to hold on. Remember that life goes on no matter what.

Clouds and weather are like the people that come into our life for a short passage of time . They come and go while some people are like the sky, they remain constant. Clouds and weathers are mere guests in the sky that vanishes leaving behind the sky. Yet, the sky survives alone.

CHAPTER FOURTEEN

Selfless sacrifice

We often see people around us busy working in their own ways and we think it is normal to be that way. However, how often do we reach out and enquire if they need help? It is often rare, because we are so busy even for ourselves that we overlook others. We only dedicate our time to earn our living whilst sacrificing our health and energy without realising that we cannot use it to buy another lifetime.

We ignorantly carry on with our lives also wasting time without realising that we can reach out to someone and help them in some way. We may feel like we are not the right person but it is when we put ourselves in the service of others by sacrificing whatever we can, we actually find a sense of fulfilment and the meaning of integration in our life.

Looking back, I mostly had friends who were way older than me and were in the most successful paths of their life. They have beautiful career and even wonderful life partners. However in my observation, one's growth and progress with which comes a sense of fulfilment does not end there. We reach our full maturity and attain a sense of satisfaction in life only when we look out for people who need us and our concerns go beyond ourselves. Even if we are well paid for the work we do, we still remain trivial as long as we work for ourselves. We start to grow within and find deeper meaning of life only when we begin to be compassionate towards people's sorrows and struggles. It is only then we realise the true essence of peace and happiness into our life

By sacrificing ourselves to serve others we also make their life more fulfilling, meaningful, purposeful and worthwhile. In doing so, it's not only the attention and generosity but your heart goes out to them. Hence, it changes the course of your life by finding a greater meaning to life and positively contributes to others. You are not depleted when you give yourself away in service; instead it expands your joy and satisfaction. Inner peace, deeper meaning of life and joy is what you will accomplish then.

When you are compassionate and selfless towards others, you give a piece of yourself of what you are. When you share, you do not lose. Rather, you are blessed. Remember that kindness costs nothing. You can give your time, support, love and companionship to people in need, it can turn out to be a mighty help in their life.

CHAPTER FIFTEEN

Forgive and heal your Soul

The journey of life offers us many experiences on its path. But no matter the circumstances, you can always envisage them as learning phases of life. Some people like to help you grow in the name of love without actually realising that growth comes with a cost. It leads you to tremendous anxiety and resentments. Often, we tend to lose ourselves when we keep things within ourselves. However, with time we come to learn and accept that certain things cannot be changed. So we heal ourselves and forgive the people that have hurt us. Sometimes your forgiveness would not be sufficient for them. Instead it will become a standing joke for some which might cause you voluntary emotional damage.

You cannot stop bad things and moments from happening to you, so you have to adapt yourself to the situations and deal with it, as they are not your identity. The situations come and go like a flash of light and the interesting thing about being hurt is that, the more you are hurt; it only makes you stronger. The deeper you are hurt, the faster you grow.

Hold yourself up together just for some time and deal with it both physically and mentally. Give yourself some gentle support and allow yourself to express whatever you're feeling or going through. It is important to know how it feels like when some beautiful things hurt us the most. Your offenders may have done terrible things against you which might have hurt you badly. They might have done with the sole intention of hurting you or may not have meant any harm at all. But the fact is that, you being hurt and keeping it all to yourself would only bring harm and self-destruction.

We are told forgive and forget as it gives us immense joy, peace, and self-satisfaction. But we must also know that forgiveness and healing is truly realised when we have to accept and live with the person that hurts us repeatedly. Time will always test us but the only thing that truly matters is how we choose to be affected, be it negative or positive.

Free yourself of hatred for anyone from your heart so that you will not be burdened. Instead, choose to forgive people and cherish the good things about them. Let go of the bad memories you carry inside you and then peace will prevail. Set out yourself in a truth seeking journey both externally and internally and most importantly always be willing to forgive things and difficult realities about life and the truth will not withheld from you, as when we truly believe and forgive things, good things always finds its way.

Remember that healing hurts more than wounds sometimes, but we discover ourselves on the journey.

CHAPTER SIXTEEN

Harsh truth

"No matter what you do, People will always pull your leg be it good or bad".

The one whom you trust the most will be the one to stab you in your back. Innocent, kind-hearted and honest person are used more and they are the ones who get hurt the most almost all the time. Usually what can really hurt you is not what you hate but what you love. A person who instantly replies to us is free for us all day, whereas a person who always ignores us is the one whom we want to talk or prioritize.

A person who calls you on your birthday is just doing nothing whereas a person who just puts your picture and achievements in their story /time-line and wishing you is your true friend. A person who's alive gets love and care but up to some limits, where as when the same person dies receives more people's sympathy and love.

And the list goes on and on without a full stop. We don't value the things that we have and we can't undo. It is human nature that even after knowing what we will pay if we lose it yet, we don't value things even when we have it. We go for the things that are hard to catch, because getting them somewhere satisfies our ego and we attach it to our achievements.

We don't give exclusivity to those who give exclusivity to us, because we think that we have now are in a safe zone and we're not gonna lose them.

Remember! Even after having so many toys at home, how we still used to cry over a balloon that were seen on the road. We used to cry for hours for a toy, we play with it yet again that new toy becomes old for us after a day or two!

Multiple thought in our heads going on and on...... Something's work out and something's doesn't. We love very few and very few truly loves us; we expect something but receives the unexpected. Days & months pass by and so do years. With happiness, sorrow, failure, losing of loved ones and very little success yet life goes on.

Occasionally in life the unutterable moments, things and feelings which cannot be explained by the combination of letters or words; their meaning can only be perceived by the inaudible language of heart. Every individual has the opportunity to Change things making a positive difference and learn to live up despite of all the things one has endure on the past. "Things don't always go the way we plan, so be prayerful for the things you love and for the person you are no matter where you walk" Dad, used to tell me this, though I truly never understood it until, life taught me the hard way.

No matter how hard or painful it is, learn to swallow when it's the harsh truth of life and accept that there are certain things you can't change. Don't confuse it with accepting abusive behaviour but accept the truth of people's feeling and thing's. In the end you will realize that it's all meaningless. Our endless endeavour to get rich, getting worked up, wanting attention, life and likes as it say that "All is Vanity ". So start appreciating the things and learn to forgive and be grateful for the life you have while acknowledging what you have.

CHAPTER SEVENTEEN

Come what may, Love it

In the midst of living ordinary lives, we face challenges beyond our thoughts. Some makes us cry, some makes us laugh. Some moments seem beautiful only to discover that it wasn't. Nevertheless, some moments are unpleasant until we realise that those were the best things that made us stronger and wiser. There are even times in life when you don't find any purpose and we begin to question our existence, unaware of those purposes. At times, life knocks us down and we lose our hope and stop believing on certain things.

Everyone battles through life. The only difference is we all fight different battles better known to ourselves. During this time of battle, all we can do is to be strong and never stop believing because hope is never lost. We ought to hold on and not let go like they say "nothing lasts forever" and that's a good thing.

Every time you lose hope, always remember and remind yourself that you are a fighter. You never know what tomorrow holds. Likewise, know that you are stronger than you think and you can get through anything. Follow the light, don't give up and don't give in, as this day too shall pass. Everything has its end that is the destiny of everything and all kind. You are going to be okay, just have courage and believe in yourself.

You are going to lose things, and lose people you really love and care about. However, not everything is under our control and it is okay to be that way. There are many things that we can't explain. Often, things happen unexpectedly and we are forced to deal with it. There are people in our mind that we think of everyday but are no longer present in our lives. We have to learn to accept the reality and go on with our lives, to find our purpose and figure things out. Everybody knows how much you smile and keep your head up, not knowing that there's pain and misery underneath. But nothing ever stays the same, so does our pain, it always gets better. Everybody has the opportunity to change things and rise above by making positive progress.

You cannot control everything that happens to you but, you can always overcome anything that happens to you. There will be days you get up in the morning and things aren't the way you hoped they would be. There will be times when people will disappoint you or let you down. But that is when you have to remind yourself that things will get better. Get further by trusting your own judgement and opinions. It may not be easy at times, however, in these times of struggle you will find a strong sense of who you are because the challenges and changes will always help you to find your own path that you know are meant to come true. Apparently, when days are filled with frustration and unexpected events, believe in yourself and all you want your life to be.

CHAPTER EIGHTEEN

Explore yourself and live your own

Many of us live a common life. We are surrounded by people with almost the same thinking, a more common ground and profession around us. There is nothing wrong with any of that. However, if we think beyond, not everyone is the same in aims and visions. Some of us want to follow our own passion, sticking to our own paths. On the other hand, a large group of people give up their dreams intimidated by the thoughts that they will not be accepted by the society. Hence, their dreams are rather what their parents or academics want them to be. Following someone else's passion will not get you anywhere close to your passion.

Often we get asked about what we want to be. And we often get advices from people according to their perception on what they want us to be, what work or profession we must pursue, which field will pay off the high package or which things fit us the most. Many at times, what they wanted and want us to be is not something we want and wanted to be. This is a common discouragement among people, especially the youths. The youths detach themselves from the things and visions they once valued and loved as they lack support into the things they wanted and get the most support into the things they don't.

I have come across people in my life that give up on their dreams and follows their parents' or some other person's advice. When asked whether they are happy with what they do, sadly, no one was proud of what they did or do. Instead they regret not following their hopes and dreams envisioned for themselves. As by nature, we humans never get satisfied with what we have already, we always want more and more and I don't think there's enough of anything that can satisfy our wants.

Nobody knows us better than we know ourselves. No one knows why we want to be something we want to be, and that is actually the power we have of ourselves to choose the things we want and to go after the things we desire. It is better to live our own, the way we want to but not how others want us to be. As at the end of the day, it is our own life and we are our own responsibility. There are moments in life when we hate the fact that life itself is a series of decision, because with everything we choose to be, we are also leaving behind a choice. But then I believe it is better to choose what we want to or how we want to live, even if we are afraid of making the wrong choices or not making a choice at all.

CHAPTER NINETEEN

Follow your intuition

Life is much greater than we thought and we are much more capable than we think we are. If we look around today, the ideas and innovations, every little thing manufactured, invented, everything was just somebody else's idea until he/she practically worked towards it.

Inside each one of us, we have a burning desire to do things and there are so many things yet to be discovered within ourselves. One can always choose to trust in what you believe and try it out without fears. Apparently, you have been listening to what you should and shouldn't for most of your life. Most importantly, be willing enough to face setbacks, failures and have the courage to walk your way without giving up, in order to bring out the best in you. Do not depend on luck. Luck is all about you being at the right place at the right time, and not everyone can get lucky. Luck is either God's blessings or lessons.

Always remember that what you have inside you is much more than what you are now. So explore it, set up your mind and go for it. It will for sure test everything you have in you. However, if you just go on with the process of loving your ways, long enough it will reward you one day, one way or the other. Nothing in life comes easy. There is a price to be paid for everything you do. And when you pay, you learn and grow. All the great leaders who are remembered for their works, the ones that we see today, are not just by luck or by chance, but through hard work, consistency and dedication.

Don't let anything or anyone influence you where you should go. The world is full of opinions and directions that let you forget what you are destined for. Focus on yourself, even if you fail never stop working and believing. Always remind yourself that you are born for something worth remembering. Life is not just about existing but for living and exploring what lies beneath and beyond us; to write our own story, to inspire people around us through our works, action and deeds. Life can be a lonely road before you even start doing something you love. That is one reason why so many people give up and feel like their ideas of doing something they love is not good enough or worth it.

But the fact is that, when you focus in yourself by doing and following the things you love, you are actually transforming yourself from someone who does things to get people's attention, to someone who gets attention from people by inspiring what you do. It is very important for us to understand ourselves by spending time on what we want to follow and how we can bring an impact not only to ourselves but in other people's life too.

We can always inspire people through our works so that it isn't always about understanding ourselves but people understanding themselves too. Stop depriving yourself of things you believe will bring something better for your life, instead give yourself permission to enjoy and try all the things you always believed in. Life is too short not to live the way you envisioned. You don't know how bad something is until you try something better, so stop holding others responsible for your deeds and start being accountable to your own deeds. Have faith and follow the things you love and no matter what you go through. Take a step and document everything you have learnt along the journey. Further down the line, you can look back and celebrate the gains, how they become a part of your story but not the end of your story.

CHAPTER TWENTY

Self-Education

Life is the real classroom. You truly understand life and the real world once you understand that the greatest value in life is learning and living each day of your life practically. Self learning will lead you far more than formal education because it is a never ending process. It goes on even when you fail to achieve or succeed at something. Life will teach you the greatest things and the worst thing as well. We are to educate ourselves by learning from our own lives. What you learn through formal education is just what you learn from someone who has learned from someone else.

You obtain the knowledge but not experience and the value, and it is all about how much you can obtain into you through them and use them practically. There is nothing wrong with that even so, you must understand that formal education today hardly enables us to make a living. It will not teach you how to be mentally stable, how to find purpose and live up to that. It is more like a trend if we look deeply as there are limits to how far you can go and what position you will hold and that you cannot assure if we look at today's society. It is all about who the bigger dog is until and unless you are making use of what you have learned, or else everything seems to be a piece of paper or a collection of numbers.

Looking back, at some point in life, we were all told that the only way to succeed and liberate a person's life is through education. However, it is partially true. Since we are taught and raised that way, we focus only on it not even caring about the importance and purpose of our lives. We were fixated and programmed in such a way that we consider this is the only way out for success. And it seems to me that the only reason behind this concept is because people are not self-educated.

We spend more than 20 years of our lifetime and even more only to find out later that what we learned, the certificates handed out, were all just mere papers until and unless you make use of it. Also, once you get there, nobody cares about your certificate and educational qualifications. All they assume is your work and how much you earn and nothing more than that. The real truth is, it is not about how much you have learned or how many degrees you hold. However it is more about what you do or what you have achieved and most importantly are you willing to make use of what you have learned. At the end of the day, people will hardly remember any of your educational degrees or your good/bad deeds.

Education will lift you up to some level to compete education against education but it is incapable to use and match up with life. Give much importance to self-education as much as you do with formal education. The value of self exploring is much more ahead than education. When you learn more about yourself by exploring, you not only learn about certain things but you get to learn what is really inside of you, update about various things required for living life practically. It will help you become a better version of yourself and give you the freedom to explore, learn everything you wanted which does not fit in formal education.

"Formal education means one size fits all."

Education is neither about going to college nor having a degree; it comes in everything you do. The way we treat people, the way we see things and beyond. So, the real definition of education is to build up a process of solving real life problems and reaching out by extending our hand.

CHAPTER TWENTY-ONE

Be What You are

As a school boy growing up, I can clearly recall who I was and what I wanted to be. The saddest part of it was that, I don't really remember asking myself who I truly want to be? What I wanted to achieve back then? For all those years, wanting to be this and that was never my thought. Instead I was admiring people's way of living without really knowing what I would love to do when I grow up and what kind of person I wanted to actually become. It was merely a dream. That was me not knowing who I really was but living someone's reflection without asking myself.

Furthermore, for years my fears and thoughts of how others would perceive me, for being me grew bigger. I remember being discouraged to go to class because of my average height. I was laughed at for being short and little and sometimes even bullied. Most of the time I was afraid even to go to new places and meet new people, as there were thoughts and flashbacks constantly running through my mind, of people mocking at me for being me. I was afraid that I wasn't myself. Many at times, I simply wanted to create a face, just to show that everything was good and ok and that I love what people had to say about me but deep down I was hurting. The "me " I felt in my heart had become so small and so far away from who I was, until I begin to take little piece of myself back into one, by gathering all the courage to find myself all over again. I started focusing more on what I see myself as a person but not how others see me. It was not easy, it was not always fun, and it was not quick but looking back and remembering what I did to overcome all of those fears and challenges was something I did it for myself.

Most people suffer from identity crisis without even knowing who they really are. Normalizing that it is okay to be someone we are not, to protect ourselves just for a moment is never okay. "Be yourself " is not just simple words but it is about learning and knowing to live with our own flaws and imperfection, without fears, and most importantly understanding that what we are is what makes us who we are, without trying to live up like someone else.

Identity is one of the root causes of our challenges from my experiences and understanding. If we look deeply within ourselves, most of us play roles of people, leaving aside our own. We fake that we are okay even when we are not. We mask ourselves out of fear to be judged; which is not really us, we pretend to be someone we are not, and even more, we try to achieve certain things that we don't really need, to impress people. That is how we end up living a life that is not our own. When we try to understand ourselves, who we truly are, it is often hard as we feel like we are losing everything of ourselves. We fake being someone we are not for a long time, we think that it is our own and find it hard to let go.

When we lack a stable sense of self, we don't really understand what we feel. To deal with our own feelings and emotions we need to understand them at the first place, by knowing who we are as a person. It should be followed by our actions to eliminate and recreate genuine connections with ourselves in every way and relearn how to love ourselves, to fully accept as we are with our own identity.

One thing I've learned was that, never to seek the acceptance of others because when you do, you lose acceptance with yourself. Do not hide anything and do not shy away from things, do not follow anything that is not yours. I believe being yourself is learning to be okay with the person you are. It is about authenticity and owning things as a person and not by something we aren't. It also means to live life on your terms and conditions by knowing that you are the narrator and the protagonist to your story. Stop worrying about what others think of you. Focus on yourself first, then other people.

CHAPTER TWENTY-TWO

The Power of Words

One of the most powerful tools you have within yourself is none other than your own words. It has the power of life and death as in, the capability to kill and heal a person with your words. They are both a blessing and a curse when you know how to use them. The right words spoken at the right time and tone can heal someone. Likewise, harsh and rude words spoken to people can destroy them physically, emotionally and mentally. The injuries to a body can be seen but it fades away with time, yet the injuries of the heart caused by words can accrue with time.

If we look around today, it is interesting to know that many people are blessed with the ability to put their thoughts and ideas into words. However, many do not understand the value and the power of their words. They simply speak out what they feel like and what they think is the best from their point of view, without giving a second thought. It is important to know how not to underestimate the power of words. Words are not just simply words alone but it carries meaning. We realise its deep meaning when we understand that they can humiliate, destroy a person or a situation.

There is a saying "Be careful with your words, once they are said they can only be forgiven not forgotten". Words itself is a reminder to use them very carefully. You may be forgiven for what you have said but the words you use against them will always hold them back at some point. A word once spoken out of your mouth have the ability to build up or tear up, to lift people higher or to drag them down, to inspire or achieve something great, to push them down to mediocrity, to motivate or to inspire, all because of the word that comes out of your mouth. They do not only influence others but also influence you. Your words are something that remains and it will set you free or lock you up or condemn you. So be careful with the words you say.

Something my dad always remind me and my brother is, "Choose your words wisely", "be careful with the words you say ", "n this world even if we speak only the good things, there would still be left with many more to speak the goodness again". To think before speaking is something that not everyone can follow up. Down the line, I have hurt and I have been hurt by words. The meaning of a small word has more power than the biggest sophisticated words you can think of in your value. Think of all those people who have had the strength and encouragement because of the words spoken to them.

At the same time, also think about all those people who have had their dreams, hopes and lives crushed all by the words spoken to them. We spill out so many harsh words when we are angry, sometimes when we don't even mean it. We simply release everything we think of without giving a break only to ponder later and end up regretting for our action. However, no amount of regret can help reverse the moment and the words that spilled out, for they are etched onto someone's heart deeply. Even though you mend with the same person by forgiving each other, the words will be remembered and will live on unceasingly to both the individuals involved.

You can only have control over your words as long as they are confined to yourself. Once they come out of your mouth, they pose as destruction or a wreaking havoc. Remember that your words may have more power over people; however, not every two person is same. Sometimes we think we won't hurt someone but may end up becoming something that really does. So be aware of your words and actions and be thankful for being blessed with the ability to speak your heart out.

Regardless of everything you have read in this book, if you have taken away something positive than I'll be very grateful. Lastly, I urge all the readers that, "You should never be afraid of doing the things you love."

Yimkumer .

9 798887 496177

Printed by Libri Plureos GmbH in Hamburg, Germany